STEAM & Me™
PUPPIES

K. A. ROE

Starry Forest Books

SCIENCE · TECHNOLOGY · ENGINEERING · ARTS · MATHEMATICS

Draw a super-smart robot. Create your own wind energy. Find out if your teeth are as sharp as a shark's. Go back in time to the world of dinosaurs or rocket into space. Power up that scientific brain of yours with STEAM&Me!

Photos, facts, and fun hands-on activities fill every book. Explore and expand your world with science, technology, engineering, arts, and math.

STEAM&Me is all about you!

Great photos to help you get the picture

New ideas sure to change how you see your world

How Puppies Grow
Most puppies are fully grown by the time they are about one year old. But they still need you!

Puppies and kids go together like sunshine and sunglasses!

You and your puppy are a perfect pair.

Adopting a little puppy is a very big deal. Puppies need a lot of care! They need to be fed, walked, trained, and brushed. When they're sick, they need to be taken to the vet. Puppies also need to be played with and loved. Even if you don't have a dog, you can help friends or neighbors with their dogs.

Dog Docs
Veterinarians are doctors who take care of animals.

STEAM&Me — Help your puppy stay healthy. Some ideas: Brush your puppy's teeth once a week. Keep her skin and coat healthy by brushing her often. And when brushing or petting your puppy, pay attention to any changes. Does she have any new lumps or bumps? If so, let a grown-up know.

28

29

Fascinating facts to fill and thrill your brain

Hands-on activities to spark your imagination

Woof!

Welcome to the world of puppies! There are so many dogs in the world: big dogs, little dogs, furry dogs, and even hairless dogs. And all dogs start out as adorable puppies. In this book you will learn all about puppies, how they grow up to be dogs, and why humans call dogs our best friends.

How Puppies Grow

A puppy's most important job is growing! In just one year, puppies go from tiny, helpless babies to full-grown adults. A puppy is constantly learning and changing. In boxes like these, you will learn how puppies grow into adult dogs.

Someday this roly-poly ball of fur will grow up. Our job is to help her become a friendly and healthy adult dog.

Puppies are so much fun! In boxes like these, you will explore ways humans and puppies are the same or different.

Coyote

Dingo

African wild dog

While canines share traits, they may look and act very different from each other.

Dogs are part of the canine family.

Dogs and their puppies are related to wolves. Scientists think they share an **ancestor**. That's a relative that lived a long time ago. Dogs are also related to coyotes, dingoes, and wild dogs. They are all part of the same family of animals known as *canines*.

How Puppies Grow

Both mother dogs and mother wolves carry their puppies for about nine weeks before giving birth.

Canine Crews

Wolves, coyotes, and wild dogs live in groups called *packs*. Packs are like family and friends who live and hunt together. A pet dog's pack includes its humans.

Can a **PERSON** be a **PUPPY'S best friend?**

Dogs and people go way back. Some scientists believe puppies began living with humans more than 40,000 years ago! Dogs probably first helped humans by barking and scaring off other animals. And humans helped their new besties by giving them food.

How Puppies Grow

A puppy's brain is open to new learning experiences during the dog's first 12 to 16 weeks after birth. It's really important for puppies to meet lots of friendly people during that time so they'll feel comfortable and happy around people when they grow up.

Ancient cave paintings show dogs working and living with humans long ago. Draw a picture of a dog living and working with humans today.

STEAM&Me

Dogs at Work

Dogs do many jobs for humans. Some work as police dogs, guide dogs, actor dogs, service dogs, soldier dogs—and, of course, best friends!

Dogs and humans depend on each other.

There are so many puppies!

There are more than 300 dog **breeds**, or types, in the world. Dog breeds come in all shapes and sizes. Different dog breeds have different features, like pointy or rounded snouts, long or short hair, or different patterns on their coats. Sometimes, a breed of dog has a special job it can do. The Australian cattle dog breed can **herd** cows and other farm animals.

Marvelous Mutts

Dogs that are more than one breed—or no breed—are called *mutts*. Mutts are the most popular dogs in the United States. In fact, some people call mutts the All-American Dog!

A basset hound's long ears sweep scents toward its nose, so basset hounds are super smellers. An Alaskan malamute is strong and has warm fur for cold weather, so they make excellent sled dogs. What talents do *you* have that make you good at something? Are you a fast runner, so you're good at sports? Are your taste buds extra sharp, so you're a good cook?

STEAM & Me

Big, small, fluffy, smooth, floppy-eared, and pointy-eared—they are all puppies!

How Puppies Grow

This puppy looks a lot like its mother dog. The puppy has her coloring. If both parent dogs are the same breed, the puppy will probably look a lot like both of them. If a puppy's parents are from different breeds, she may look and act more like one than the other.

Dogs can be very, very large or very, very small!

Huge Dogs
Irish wolfhounds can weigh up to 180 pounds.

Teeny-Tiny Dogs
Teacup poodles can weigh as little as 2 pounds.

12

Puppies come in all sizes.

A newborn puppy might be as small as a golf ball. Or a newborn puppy might weigh as much as 2 pounds and be as big as a pineapple. The shortest adult dog ever recorded was a Chihuahua named Milly. She was less than 4 inches tall, about the height of a crayon, and weighed just 1 pound. The tallest dog was a Great Dane named Zeus. He weighed 155 pounds and was 44 inches tall, which is taller than a mailbox.

How Puppies Grow

Puppies double their weight in their first two weeks of life. At three months old, they can be up to four times the size they were at birth.

Learn puppy talk.

Because puppies can't talk, they must communicate in other ways. Dogs use **body language** and sounds to let other dogs and humans know what's on their mind. They might bark when they want to play or growl when they want to be left alone. Dogs also communicate through smells.

How Puppies Grow

Mother dogs talk to their puppies with yips, growls, and body language. Puppies also learn to communicate by playing with their littermates.

Think of ways you communicate without talking. When you are mad, do you frown? Do you cry when you are sad? How do you show other people that you are happy? Look into a mirror and make faces to show that you are happy, sad, mad, scared, bored, and excited. Can you move your body in ways that show the same feelings?

STEAM*Me*

Excuse Me!

Sniffing each other's rear ends may look rude, but it's how dogs learn important information about each other.

Yaaawn

Yawning doesn't always mean a puppy is tired. It may mean she is nervous.

This puppy lets her friend know she'd like to play by **bowing**.

Go, puppy, go!

Puppies are built to run! Their four legs work together to move them forward quickly. They have great balance and can turn around fast. Some dogs, like greyhounds, can run very fast. Other dogs, like dalmatians, can run very long distances.

How Puppies Grow

When puppies are born, they can't see, hear, smell, or walk. They take their first steps at around two weeks old.

Dogprints

Paw pads protect puppy feet and help them stop quickly. Dog nails help them dig, of course. But they also help them grip. A dog can steady a bone it's chewing with its paw and nails.

Puppies have super snouts.

The *snout* is an important part of a dog's body. It's where you'll find the dog's nose and mouth. Without a snout, a dog couldn't eat, drink, smell, or keep from overheating.

How Puppies Grow

It's normal for puppies to chew on things as their teeth are growing in. You can keep a puppy safe and your things safe by putting away your items and keeping them off the floor.

When you get too hot, your body cools off through sweating. You might feel sweat in your armpits or on your forehead. To understand how sweat cools you, wet a cotton ball and touch it to the skin on your arm. Then blow air on your arm. Which part feels cooler, the wet part of your arm or the dry part of your arm?

STEAM & Me

Stop

Muzzle

A dog's or puppy's snout starts at the *stop*, which is the name for the place where its forehead meets its *muzzle* (another word for snout).

No Sweat!

Dogs don't cool themselves by sweating like humans do. Instead, they cool off by panting with their tongues.

What big teeth you have, pup!

Dog teeth are made to tear and rip, and to grind food. Dogs have a set of 42 teeth, and each kind of tooth has a special use.

Although many dogs eat dry pet food called kibble, they can also eat meat and some plants. They have pointy teeth for ripping and flatter molars for grinding.

Minty Clean!
Puppies need their teeth brushed just like people do!

How Puppies Grow

Like human babies, puppies are born with no teeth and then grow a set of 28 baby teeth. By the time a puppy is 6 or 7 months old, its baby teeth have fallen out and been replaced by 42 grown-up teeth. Puppy teeth are called milk teeth, but they are sharp as pins!

Puppies have some super-cool features that increase their sense of smell. Their wet noses help catch more scent molecules.

How Puppies Grow

New puppies can't yet see or walk, but they can already smell their mother's milk.

Puppies have spectacular sniffers, too.

Dogs have an amazing sense of smell—which means puppies do, too. A dog's sense of smell is up to 100 thousand times more sensitive than a human's! Dogs smell so well, they can sense a tablespoon of coffee in an Olympic-sized pool.

Nose to the Rescue

Because dogs have such a strong sense of smell, they often use it to help humans. Sniffer dogs find missing people, detect weapons, and even sniff out cancer.

Sniff a cookie. What do you smell? A puppy doesn't just smell the cookie. She can also smell all the ingredients. Can you smell the different parts of a cookie like a puppy can? Try to smell everything that was used to make the cookie. Check your guesses against the ingredients list.

And what big **EYES** you have!

Dogs' eyes work differently from the way humans' eyes do. Dogs are color blind, so they can't see all the colors that we do. Most dogs can't see as far as humans can. But dogs' eyes can do some things better than humans' eyes. Dogs are better at seeing fast-moving things. They also see better at night.

How Puppies Grow

When a puppy is first born, its eyes are tightly closed. They stay that way until the puppy is about two weeks old. A puppy's eyesight is very poor at first. By about eight weeks old, most puppies see as well as adult dogs.

Third eyelid

Puppies have a **third eyelid** that protects the puppy's eye by clearing away debris. It also provides an extra layer of protection against dirt, food scraps, snow, or rain—or anything else that might fly into the puppy's eye.

Different dog breeds can have different ear shapes on the outside. But the insides of their ears are mostly the same.

Listen up, pup.

Dogs hear much better than humans do. For example, what you can hear across one playground, some dogs can hear four playgrounds away! If you've ever noticed that your dog seems to know when people are coming to the door even before they arrive, that's why. Dogs can also hear sounds humans can't at all, such as high-pitched whistles and maybe even a coming earthquake.

How Puppies Grow

Did you know that newborn puppies can't hear? Their ears are very small and close to their heads. They only begin to hear at two to three weeks old, when their ears develop. Until then, they rely on their sense of smell.

What Did You Say?

Have you seen a puppy's ears suddenly go from loose and relaxed to pointing straight up? That puppy adjusted its ears for better hearing. The 18 muscles in puppies' ears help puppies move their ears to pick out important sounds.

How Puppies Grow

Most puppies are fully grown by the time they are about one year old. But they still need you!

Dog Docs

Veterinarians are doctors who take care of animals.

Puppies and kids go together like sunshine and sunglasses!

You and your puppy are a perfect pair.

Adopting a little puppy is a very big deal. Puppies need a lot of care! They need to be fed, walked, trained, and brushed. When they're sick, they need to be taken to the vet. Puppies also need to be played with and loved. Even if you don't have a dog, you can help friends or neighbors with their dogs.

STEAM+Me

Help your puppy stay healthy. Some ideas: Brush your puppy's teeth once a week. Keep her skin and coat healthy by brushing her often. And when brushing or petting your puppy, pay attention to any changes. Does she have any new lumps or bumps? If so, let a grown-up know.

So many puppies!

In this book you've learned so much about dogs and puppies and ways to help the puppies you meet grow into healthy adult dogs. Match the puppies to the pictures of their breeds shown earlier in this book. Choose your favorite, while you're at it! Draw a picture of you and your perfect pup. What would it look like? What jobs could it do? What's its name?

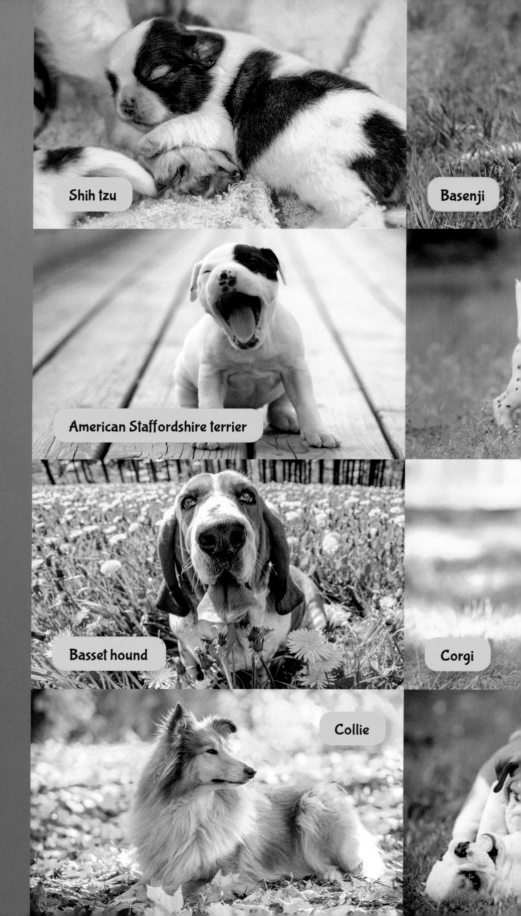

Shih tzu

Basenji

American Staffordshire terrier

Basset hound

Corgi

Collie

American pit bull terrier

Cocker spaniel

Dalmatian

Greater Swiss mountain dog

Australian shepherd

Irish wolfhound

Labrador retriever

English bulldog

Chocolate Labrador retriever

French bulldog

31

Glossary

Learn these key words and make them your own!

ancestor: a relative from the past. *Dogs and wolves may share an* ancestor.

body language: movements that show how a person or animal is feeling or what they are thinking. *A puppy's* body language *can show you when it wants to play.*

breed: a type of an animal that shares characteristics. *German shepherds are my favorite* breed *of dog.*

herd: to keep animals together in a group. *Some dogs* herd *sheep.*

kibble: dry pet food. *My dog loves* kibble *for breakfast.*

STEAM & Me and Starry Forest® are trademarks or registered trademarks of Starry Forest Books, Inc. • Text and Illustrations © 2020 and 2021 by Starry Forest Books, Inc. • This 2021 edition published by Starry Forest Books, Inc. • P.O. Box 1797, 217 East 70th Street, New York, NY 10021 • All rights reserved. No part of this publication may be reproduced, stored in a retrieval system, or transmitted in any form or by any means (including electronic, mechanical, photocopying, recording, or otherwise) without prior written permission from the publisher. • ISBN 978-1-946260-93-2 • Manufactured in China • Lot #: 2 4 6 8 10 9 7 5 3 1 • 03/21